Dyslexia:

Then &

Now

To Sue
Hope you enjoy the read.
Love + Blessings
Elian

First published in UK – 2022

© E. Davies - Activate M.W. Publishing

Original Copyright holder – El. Davies

ISBN - 9798836438586

DEDICATION

I would like to dedicate this book to….

Mum & Dad for believing in me and encouraging me not to give up through the good and bad times, for believing in my potential.

Mrs Mandy Kingdom for teaching me key building blocks and techniques to help navigate my journey through education.

Mrs Val Evans for being the best English teacher I ever had, for seeing my potential, for helping to rebuild my confidence, and teaching me that I could succeed in English and ultimately inspiring me to reach for my ambition of being an author.

Mrs Marina Hughes for being an inspiring Technology and Catering teacher, for developing my passion for cooking and textiles, for helping to rebuild my self confidence and self-belief. For always believing in my full potential both academically and personally.

ENDORSEMENTS

"It was a privilege to read through an early draft of El's book – both informative and inspiring at the same time. I hope that the personal journey so bravely shared by El, and all that she has achieved since, including as an author and business owner, serves to inspire those that follow.

As a school, we are fortunate to benefit from a number of skills that El brings to her role and the wider community. Some of these are strengths arising from her dyslexia, others are character traits, such as resilience that she has developed to ensure she is not held back; the combination is a strong one, leading to a much-valued colleague within our community".

Paul Vicars - Headteacher

"I found this book to be informative, inspiring and one I want to recommend to anyone who is interested in learning, education, child development, or people in general!...

...This book is perfectly structured to inform someone new to this topic about all aspects of dyslexia. It is also detailed enough to deepen the knowledge of anyone experiencing dyslexia or supporting anyone who is, either in a professional or personal capacity.

At the heart of the book is the spirit of determination and enquiry embodied by El. I am sure everyone who reads this will come away feeling better informed, uplifted, and determined to help themselves and those around them overcome any obstacles to self-improvement.

I endorse this work whole-heartedly".

Mr. Gez Flowers – Former Head of School.

"The over-riding message I got from El's book is that teachers can have a long-lasting impact on a young person's progress and general self-esteem, both positive and negative. As teachers, we have a responsibility to look for talent rather than deficiencies, and should seek to provide opportunities to maximise potential, instead of putting obstacles in the way. It is to El's great credit that she has shown the mental fortitude to overcome these barriers, but it still raises questions about why it was made so difficult".

Mr. Pete Lindberg – Head of Science & Chemistry

"This well-researched and informative account of a life which could have been blighted by dyslexia proves that with support from parents, teachers, and professionals, together with a determination and doggedness to succeed, hurdles can not only be overcome, but also a fruitful career can be attained. El takes the reader on a journey from childhood to adulthood, where she encounters numerous difficulties which could throw her off course. Yet she always finds ways of achieving; she is resilient, inventive, ambitious, and courageous. As someone who knew little about the specific symptoms, diagnosis and treatment of dyslexia this book is a real eye opener."

Ruth Daly – Former Teacher

"El has refused to be defined by dyslexia. Rather, through dogged persistence and a refusal to settle for less than her best, she has reached beyond the expectations placed upon her by others. Let her story inspire you to do the same".

Garry & Kim Halliday

"This book starts with a very good, comprehensive explanation about Dyslexia and follows with El's extremely encouraging personal story. Her determination, strength and refusal to give up or be written off will inspire others to overcome as well".

Melanie Tyrrell – Teacher, South Africa

CONTENTS

FOREWORD

INTRODUCTION

PART 1   THEN AND NOW

CHAPTER 1   DYSLEXIA THEN AND NOW

CHAPTER 2   WHAT IS DYSLEXIA?

PART 2   BEFORE KNOWING

CHAPTER 3   EARLY EDUCATION

CHAPTER 4   SEEKING ADVICE

CHAPTER 5   COPING WITH NEW WAYS OF

                LEARNING

PART 3   COMPREHENSIVE SCHOOL

                AND GCSEs

CHAPTER 6   STARTING COMPREHENSIVE

                 SCHOOL

CHAPTER 7   PREPARING FOR GCSEs

PART 4   ADULTHOOD EXPERIENCES

                 OF DYSLEXIA

CHAPTER 8   EARLY CAREER PATH

CHAPTER 9   KNOW AND UNDERSTAND YOUR

                 STRENGTHS

CHAPTER 10   STARTING MY OWN BUSINESS

CONCLUSION   YOU CAN DO ANYTHING YOU

                 PUT YOUR MIND TO

APPENDICES 1:   DOCUMENTARY EDUCATING

                 MANCHESTER

APPENDICES 2:   VARK MODEL

APPENDICES 3:   GLOSSARY AND USEFUL

                 INFORMATION

APPENDICES 4:   USEFUL ADDRESSES

APPENDICES 5:   REFERENCE / INFORMATIVE

BOOKS / REPORTS / PAPERS

AUTHOR BIOGRAPHY

FOREWORD

In this heart-warming and inspiring book its author, El, invites you and I, her readers, on a journey of discovery.

If you are wondering what dyslexia is - then reading El's book will take you to a place of greater knowledge.

If you are wondering how dyslexia affects people who are found to be living with this condition - then reading El's book will take you to a place of greater understanding.

If you need inspiration to find ways to overcome a hurdle in your own life, which may be dyslexia or another hurdle unique to you - then reading El's book will take you to a place of new perspective.

El begins with her own experience of the effects of dyslexia on her life as a young child and takes us through her diagnosis and on to her discovery of self-belief as she continues her journey to adulthood. As well as describing her own experiences El's work includes thorough research into the history of dyslexia and an objective overview of this complex learning difficulty which affects many people. Even if you do not live with dyslexia yourself it is very likely that you know someone who does as there are so many people who do live with this difficulty, and El's work will help you to recognise and understand their situation.

El then goes on to write in more depth about her own journey. As she describes her experiences El acknowledges the help and encouragement, she has received from many people to achieve all that she has achieved to-day. El's work is a wonderful affirmation of the importance of the gift of encouragement to anyone who may be struggling with any kind of difficulty and an inspiration to all who read this book to encourage others around us.

But perhaps the most heart- warming aspect of the book is the determination with which El approaches the challenges that she has faced and still faces and her message to all of her readers, "with hard work and determination you can succeed."

Thank you El for your remarkable and inspiring book, you have succeeded in writing an inspirational piece of work which will be a blessing to many, keep on succeeding!

Revd. Canon Christine Broad.

INTRODUCTION

Hello. My name is El Davies, and I have dyslexia. I was diagnosed with dyslexia while I was in primary school and from then until now, I have discovered true self-belief, and an understanding of my own strengths and limitations. Through my personal journey I have learnt which tips and techniques worked best for me during studying and work life.

There are now many self-help books on the market about dyslexia, which give advice on learning various tips and techniques to improve your specific learning difficulties. I am not going to profess to know the secret to your personal success - this is something you need to discover for yourself, as everyone is different; what works for me, may or may not work for you. That being said, there are some very helpful and insightful books that will explain various methods to try and work round your specific learning difficulty. I would encourage you to keep searching for the techniques that unlock your learning; some things will work for you and some won't be so helpful, but the IMPORTANT thing is to keep trying and NEVER give up!

This book is about my personal journey through life with dyslexia. It has been written as an encouragement to those of us who struggle with specific learning difficulties such as dyslexia to help you to believe in yourself, and not allow yourself to be written off by anyone whether they are parents, teachers, friends, or employers.

I began writing about dyslexia when I was just fourteen years old and some of the contents have been adapted into the narrative of this book.

My English teacher at that time was a lady named Val Evans, who genuinely believed in me and in my potential. Her enthusiasm for the English language inspired me to achieve and do well in the subject. During the time Mrs. Evans was my English teacher I wrote the first part of this book and its original draft became part of my English course work. After writing the original draft for school, I captured the vision to help others who struggle with dyslexia. I developed the first part of this book into a manuscript and wrote to Professor Tim Miles at Bangor University who headed up the dyslexia unit.

To my amazement Professor Tim Miles wrote back, saying how helpful it was to have a teenager's view on dyslexia. He was so impressed that he printed extracts in the university newsletter. He also recommended it for publishing and gave me a couple of publishing leads along with asking if he could keep a copy in the Dyslexia Units Library as a resource.

In this book I will share how dyslexia has affected me and how I have never given up, though sometimes (especially in the early days) I wanted to: when people didn't understand and tried to disregard me by saying things like I was slow or unintelligent. It is my hope this book will inspire you to keep persevering, to keep learning and to discover your way to personal success.

As someone who was given up for lost academically because of dyslexia, and whose parents were told not to expect their daughter to achieve any GCSEs let alone any other further education, I can safely say I have proved those people wrong! I attained good GCSEs, National Certificates and various Diplomas; I trained as Counsellor, a Life Coach, as well as starting my own business in Wellbeing therapies. If I can achieve my true potential and not let dyslexia hold me back, so can you!

As you read this book, I hope it will help you to understand a little more about dyslexia and how a child feels when he or she endeavours to cope with its associated problems.

I also hope that you will find it interesting, especially if you are experiencing similar difficulties or know someone else who is.

PART 1

THEN AND NOW

CHAPTER 1

DYSLEXIA THEN AND NOW

Key points in the History of Dyslexia

1877 – Adolph Kussmaul was a German physician who was the first person to diagnose "Word Blindness" / "Complete Text Blindness"

1887 – Rudolph Berlin was a German ophthalmologist who was the first person to use the term "dyslexia" to encompass reading challenges as a result of disability.

1896 – William Pringle Morgan published a work called "A Case of Congenital Word Blindness".

1917 – James Hinshelwood wrote and published as book called "Congenital Word Blindness".

1942 – Martin Attlee starts at Millfield School to try and overcome his word blindness.

1949 – In the United States of American the Orton Society was established. Now known as the International Dyslexia Association

1962 – The Invalid Children's Aid Association opened and funded the Word Blind Centre in London associated with Neurologist Mr. Macdonald Critchley and Psychologist Professor Tim Miles. This Centre brought together a few researchers who worked with individuals with the condition dyslexia.

1962 – In Parliament, dyslexia was mentioned for the first time.

1968 – The World Federation of Neurology Research Group had its first meeting on Word Illiteracy and Developmental Dyslexia took place.

1970 – Dyslexia was referred to within the "Chronically Sick and Disabled Act".

1970 – The Neurologist Macdonald Critchley wrote and published "The Dyslexic Child".

1971 – Helen Arkell, Joy Pollock and Elisabeth Waller Set up the "Helen Arkell Centre" which was based in London.

1972 – The Dyslexia Clinic was established at Barts Hospital in London by Beve' Hornsby

1972 – Doubts regarding the existence of dyslexia were voiced in the Tizard Report about children with specific learning difficulties.

1972 – The book "Specific Dyslexia" was written and published by Sandhya Naidoo; this book was one of the first major studies on dyslexia.

1972 – The Dyslexia Institute was established in London.

1972 – The British Dyslexia Association was established, and it was one of the largest, well-known organisations that champions and supports dyslexic people.

1973 – Margaret Newton established the Language and Development Unit at Aston University.

1975 – A short reference was made regarding Dyslexia in the Bullock Report entitle "A Language for Life."

1977 – At Bangor university the Bangor Dyslexia Unit was established by Professor Tim Miles and Elaine Miles which is now known as the Miles Dyslexia Centre

1978 – The Warnock Report was written regarding special education and was published.

1979 – The book called "Dyslexia: Theory and Research" was written by Frank Vellutino and published.

1987 – Dyslexia was formally recognised in the Government's parliamentary debate.

1994 – A professional body was established for individuals with a professional interest in dyslexia, this body was called "The Dyslexia Guild".

2005 – Dyslexia Action was formed by the amalgamation of The Hornsby International Dyslexia Centre and the Dyslexia Institute.

2009 – The publication of the Rose Report on Dyslexia and Literacy Difficulties.

2010 – The publication of the Equality of Work Act protecting the dyslexics in the workplace.

Overview of Dyslexia

Initially, it was believed by researchers that people who presented with the symptoms of what would later be referred to as dyslexia, thought that these people had some type of brain injury or disease which caused this condition.

In the region of 130 to 140 years have elapsed since the term 'dyslexia' was used by Rudolf Berlin; he was an ophthalmologist from Stuttgart Germany. Rudolph Berlin who noticed the difficulties some of his adult patients experienced whilst reading; yet there was no problem with the patient's vision. Rudolph Berlin concluded that their difficulties may have originated from physical change within the brain. Rudolf Berlin used a term which meant 'difficulty with words' to define the disorder.

Adolph Kussmaul, also a German and a Professor of Medicine at Strasburg, was the first to recognise the type of difficulties Berlin described, in 1877, Adolph Kussmaul called these difficulties "word-blindness". He saw that complete text blindness was present in patients,' even though the power of speech, sight, and intellect was not affected, and the children were very able apart from them having major reading difficulties. Rudolf Berlin was the first to start using the word 'dyslexia.'

UK based, James Hinshelwood who was an ophthalmologist; James Kerr a council medical officer, and William Pringle Morgan, a general practitioner focused not only on word-blindness as an isolated symptom, but these three medics also focused their work on both adults and children who presented with word-blindness. This approach undermined the previous thought of Adolph Kussmaul - that these difficulties were caused by a type of brain injury or disease that caused dyslexia in people. These three medical professionals came to the conclusion that dyslexia was NOT caused by injury or disease and so they leant towards the thought that dyslexia was congenital word-blindness.

William Pringle Morgan's and James Hinshelwood's reports about word-blindness became key to understanding the history of Dyslexia.

Peggy Anderson and Regine Meier-Hedde (2001), stated that 'This body of work became enormously significant for several reasons. First, the United Kingdom physicians wrote with a clarity and organisation that previously had not been observed in the literature. Second, they turned attention to the plight of children, and third, these physicians wrote numerous case reports on word blindness, which resulted in an accumulation of information about this enigma.'

Also, William Pringle Morgan and James Hinshelwood's role in associating dyslexia with high intelligence have had some ramifications.

Dr Samuel Torrey Orton was a neuropathologist in Iowa USA, produced his first paper on word-blindness in 1925 and submitted it to the American Neurological Association in Washington. Dr Orton referred to the original work of Kussmaul, William Pringle Morgan, and James Hinshelwood, however he came to a different line of thought based on his own case studies and clinical observations. He championed his own theory that accreted reading disorders to a lack of cerebral dominance. Dr Orton's theory redefined dyslexia as a cross-lateralisation of the brain; this meant that Dr Orton thought that the left side of the brain was doing whatever the right side of the brain would do and the left side would be functioning as the right.

Samuel Orton's theory of cerebral dominance was eventually proved to be incorrect, however, this was vital in changing the discussions regarding dyslexia toward theories of cognitive development.

Professor Tim Miles one of the most renowned researchers in dyslexia's history, thought that 'Of all the early pioneers Samuel Orton was one who, put the notion of developmental dyslexia on the map.' Samuel Orton was among the first researchers to promote phonics tuition for people with dyslexia, and today this approach is still recommended.

In the 1960s the theories about dyslexia were starting to head in the direction of cognitive development. It took a significant amount of time for dyslexia to be recognised and openly diagnosed as a condition that needs support from an early age.

In 1962 the Word Blind Centre was started under the management of Dr Alfred White Franklin and the Invalid Children's Aid Association in Bloomsbury. Others involved at the Centre were Macdonald Critchley, Oliver Zangwill, Patrick Meredith, Maisie Holt and Tim Miles.

After 1962 the beginning of modern research commenced, and as a result the Government passed legislation, which would provide protection for people with dyslexia. For example, in later years the Legislation called the Equality Act 2010.

However, an increase in the notion of dyslexia was a 'middle-class myth' that developed. This caused dyslexia to be viewed as a pseudo-medical diagnosis which was used by parents to excuse their child's reading difficulties. Alas, this argument has persisted in some areas and has been used against campaigners ever since. Initially there was a hesitancy to acknowledge dyslexia as a condition in medical, educational, and political areanas.

Under the discrepancy diagnostic model of assessment, a person was only believed to be dyslexic if they presented with a significant difference between the person's reading level and intelligence with a bias to intelligence. This historical element was an influence within the "Middle Class Myth" hypothesis that a child was nevertheless bright but had difficulty in this one area. The discrepancy model was originally relied on by organisations as a diagnostic / assessment model.

Parents with higher educational and economic levels have tended to be more aware of dyslexia in the past and to some extent to the present day.

The explanation of dyslexia's association and disassociation with particular socio-economic groups historically, cannot, then substantiate the accusations that dyslexia is a myth! There had consistently been a debate throughout history about the existence of dyslexia and a reluctance to accept it.

In 1968 The world Federation of Neurology Research Group had its first meeting on World Illiteracy and Developmental Dyslexia took place. Their definition of dyslexia was: "A disorder manifested by difficulty in learning to read even with conventional instruction, adequate intelligence and socio-cultural opportunity. It is dependent upon fundamental cognitive disabilities which are frequently of constitutional origin".

In 1970, Macdonald Critchley published "*The Dyslexic Child;*" this text pinpointed 'developmental dyslexia' was in need of urgent official consideration.

In the 1970s the condition of dyslexia was mentioned in the Chronically Sick and Disabled Persons Act. Two years later in the Tizard Report Children with Specific Reading Difficulties was said to be 'highly sceptical of the view that a syndrome of developmental dyslexia with a specific underlying cause and specific symptoms has been identified,' in light of the evidence that was emerging during this time.

1971 - Helen Arkell Dyslexia Centre was started.

1971 - The Dyslexia Clinic at Barts Hospital was founded.

In 1972 Sandhya Naidoo published "Specific Dyslexia", This was a systematic comparison of dyslexic and non-dyslexic children in Britain, and this book remains informative and interesting up to today. It concentrates on children and development in literacy; this book was one of the first major studies on Dyslexia. Sandhya Naidoo advocates early intervention and support for the dyslexic child is considerably more beneficial and fruitful than trying to rectify the problem, which becomes progressively more complicated the older a child becomes.

1972 - The British Dyslexia Association was started.

1972 - The Dyslexia Institute began.

1973 - The Language Development Unit at Aston University.

1977 - The Bangor Dyslexia Unit

In 1978 the Warnock Report was published by the then Department for Education and Science. Here, the Government's opposition to the term dyslexia was proactive.

Baroness Mary Warnock the writer of this report was advised by a senior civil servant in the Department, not to suggest that there was a special category of learning difficulty called dyslexia'. Maybe this was reflecting the reluctance to spend resources on dyslexia possibly due to the estimate of 10 percent of the population could be affected.

Post Warnock Report, the government tried to substantiate its reluctance to participate in the dyslexia debate, by voicing that it did not recognise distinctions under the term 'specific learning difficulties'.

In 1987 change was starting to occur when the government announced its interest in 'dispelling the myth'. The Government accepted dyslexia and acknowledged the importance of education progression for dyslexic children, along with the long-term welfare, successful function in adult life, and that they should receive support once identified from an early stage.

Prominent people in the field of dyslexia research include:

- Head of the Dyslexia Clinic at Barts Hospital Beve' Hornsby

- The British Dyslexia Association - Marion Welchman who was also involved in the Word Blind Centre

- Former president of the Dyslexia Institute - actress Susan Hampshire OBE - for her advocacy work.

- In 2009 the Rose Report Review, which was instructed by the Government as an independent body 'to make suggestions on how to identify and teach children with dyslexia'.

Dyslexia is a learning difficulty that predominantly affects the skills required for accurate and fluent reading and spelling.

Characteristic of dyslexia may include:

- difficulties in phonological awareness,

- verbal memory and verbal processing speed,

- Dyslexia occurs across the range of intellectual abilities.

The following co-occurring difficulties may happen alongside dyslexia but are not by themselves indicators of dyslexia.

- aspects of language,

- motor co-ordination,

- mental calculation,

- concentration,

- personal organisation,

The dyslexia debate continues in different areas primarily within educational psychology. In more recent times the book "The Dyslexia Debate" 2014 expressed criticism of the term "dyslexia" It does not question the presence of biologically based reading difficulties existing, but rather questions how best to understand and address literacy difficulties across educational, occupational, clinical, and social contexts. One of the factors limiting understanding, which was claimed in the book, is the word dyslexia, 'with respect to word-reading difficulties and suggests the "construct reading disability" is preferable for use by both researchers and clinicians. (As a lay man) I feel that the real issue isn't the title of the condition..." Dyslexia" verses "Construction Reading Disability" the issue remains a lack of understanding in the condition, not the title it had been given.

Today there remain a few different theories, which are used to explain the causes and condition of dyslexia.

There have been a few technologies which have assisted in the research of dyslexia. One of these has been the fMRI Brain SPECT imaging technologies, which have been used by doctors to enable them to view the electro-chemical functions of the brain at the same time as a patient engages with activities such as reading or rhyming exercises.

The use of these technologies provides the doctors' with an image map of the brain, which highlights the areas of function of the brain and any weak and strong areas.

The contribution of these technologies facilitated much understanding of the physical components of dyslexia.

The research carries on to find the keys that will ultimately be used in correcting or helping a dyslexic person to compensate for their specific learning difficulties.

Frequently, dyslexics experience spelling and reading difficulties, though they may also struggle with other skills like concentration, organisation, and motor coordination, so some dyslexics can present as uncoordinated and unorganised.

There is no link between intelligence and dyslexia. Individuals may be found from any intelligence level (low, average or high).

2020 – Dyslexia has received more awareness and professional support than in previous decades. Assessments and diagnosis are available for adults and children. Many charities and organisations are now available to help facilitate further understanding of dyslexia and the provision of support.

As time passes, along with the future advancement of medical, scientific, and educational research, the complexity, definitions and understandings of dyslexia will continue to be debated and evolve. Thankfully, dyslexia is now recognised as a disability through the Equality Act 2010, which adds some protection for dyslexics,

This condition does NOT affect intelligence and ability but rather presents itself as a leaning difficulty. Dyslexics now have the right to have any reasonable adjustments made either in school or the workplace. This is important because though progress has been made there is still a lot of prejudice and lack of understanding in some work and educational settings. I have experienced this in various parts of my life, but the key thing to remember is never give up and always believe in yourself.

CHAPTER 2

WHAT IS DYSLEXIA?

Dyslexia is quite a common learning difficulty, which predominantly causes problems with reading, writing and spelling. Dyslexia is a specific learning obstacle, which means it can cause problems with abilities used for traditional learning and methodologies in acquiring knowledge.

It is classified as a learning disability in law, though this condition does NOT affect intelligence and does not typically fit into a learning disability. The combining of various laws in the Equality Act 2010, does categorise dyslexia as a disability because it is an ongoing condition. The Equality Act 2010 regarding dyslexia is there to protect individuals regarding equality in work / education and the provision of reasonable adjustments for example use of overlays, Dictaphones, etc. Dyslexia is often referred to as a learning difficulty rather than disability due to dyslexia having no impact on intelligence. Dyslexia affects the way a person learns, for example a dyslexic is more likely to be a visual and kinaesthetic learner over reading and the written word.

There is not a cure or remedy for dyslexia as it is a lifelong condition, which may present challenges on a daily basis. However, a dyslexic who is given the appropriate help and support can learn to overcome a lot of the challenges that dyslexia can present and go on to be successful at school, university, and work.

It is thought that 1 in 10 people within the UK are likely to have dyslexia to some degree from mild to severe.

Indicators of Dyslexia

Frequently the signs that an individual has dyslexia will manifest when they commence school and begin to focus on acquiring the skills and abilities to read, write and spell.

These indicators can include:

- Very slow reading pace

- Very slow writing

- Confusion of the order of letters in words

- Confusion of the orders of numbers

- Writing alphabetical letters, the wrong way round, typically b and d, p and q

- Writing numbers, the wrong way round, typically 9, 6, 3.

- Poor spelling

- Inconsistent spelling

- Mirror writing – writing whole words of sentences backwards but when a mirror is held up to the words, they are able to be read.

- May have difficulty comprehending information that is written down but understands the same information when given verbally.

- Difficulty carrying out a sequence of directions.

- Difficulty remembering numbers in a sequence, for example, pin numbers and phone numbers

- Difficulty with remembering spoken / verbal instructions.

- Poor short-term memory

- Struggle with instant recall, for example difficulty recalling answers quickly i.e. teachers' questions or quiz situations

- Struggle with planning

- Struggle with organisation

- May complain of letters or words on the page appearing fuzzy, and / or moving on the page.

- May complain that they feel blinded by white paper and it is difficult to read the written work; this can also be accompanied with fuzzy or moving letters and words.

However, dyslexics frequently have excellent skills in other areas like creative thinking, problem solving, practical gifts and a keen eye for detail to name but a few.

Potential Indicators of Dyslexia at Key Life Stages

Pre-school Children

Occasionally it is possible to identify symptoms of dyslexia prior to a child commencing school.

Warning signs

- Speech development may appear delayed in comparison with children of the same age. (Comprehension)

- Difficulties with speech such as pronouncing long words correctly, for example saying "Hosbical" "Hospical" instead of Hospital. (Comprehension / Verbal)

- Challenges with expressing themselves via the spoken word; they may struggle to find the right words, or they may fail to construct sentences correctly. (Comprehension / Verbal)

- Jumbling up phrases. (Comprehension)

- Limited comprehension / appreciation / understanding of rhyming words for example cat, mat, sat, fat, hat etc. (Comprehension)

- The individual lacks interest in learning the alphabet. (Comprehension)

- Difficulty following oral commands. (Memory / Audible)

Primary school age 4-11 years old

This is the age group where dyslexia will tend to become more noticeable, as children are focusing a lot more on reading and the written word. Children can start to fall behind very quickly during this age group.

Warning signs

- May find it difficult to learn the names and sounds of letters. (Comprehension)

- Extremely poor spelling. (Comprehension / Written)

- Inconsistent and unpredictable spelling. (Comprehension / Written)

- Confusion over the order of letters within words. (Comprehension / Written)

- Very slow reading speed. (Reading / Comprehension)

- Frequently making errors when reading aloud / or finding their mind goes blank on even the simplest of words. (Reading / Comprehension)

- Very slow speed of writing. (Written)

- Poor handwriting. (Written)

- Difficulty copying written language. (Written)

- May struggle to perform a sequence of directions. (Comprehension)

- Confuses writing letters the wrong way round, for example, p instead of q, d instead of b. (Written)

- Confuses writing numbers the wrong way round, for example, 9, 6, 3, (Written)

- Very slow in the completion of their written work. (Written / Comprehension)

- Answers questions well orally but struggles writing the answers down. (Written)

- Visual disturbances that occur whilst reading, for example the individual sees the words or letters moving on the page or they appear blurred. (Visual)

- Poor phonological awareness. (Comprehension)

- Poor word attack skills. (Comprehension / Reading)

- Difficulty remembering oral instructions. (Memory / Audible)

Teenagers and Adults

This category includes all the other warning signs of dyslexia, which have been previously mentioned along with the following.

Warning Signs

- Struggles with writing reports. (Written / Planning / Organisation)

- Struggles with writing letters. (Written / Planning / Organisation)

- Struggles with planning and writing essays. (Written / Planning / Comprehension)

- Struggles with revising for examinations and tests. (Planning / Organisation)

- Extremely poor spelling. (Memory / Written / Comprehension)

- Produces poorly organised written assignments / written work, for example the individual may be deeply knowledgeable of a specific subject but has difficulty expressing that knowledge via the written word. (Planning / Organisation)

- Difficulty remembering PIN numbers. (Memory / Sequencing)

- Difficulty remembering telephone numbers. (Memory / Sequencing)

- Difficulty meeting or keeping deadlines. (Planning / Organisation)

- Struggles to take notes from lessons. (Memory / Writing / Reading)

- Struggles with taking notes from dictation / note taking. (Memory / Writing / Comprehension)

Word Attack Skills

Word attack skills refer to the ability and skill to understand and make sense of new or unfamiliar words by identifying small words or groups of letters which the individual has previously learnt.

An individual who has poor word attack skills would not be able to separate and sound out a word they have not previously read before.

An example of this would be,

"Sunday" breaking it down into "Sun" "day."

"Seaside" breaking it down into "sea" "side."

Phonological Awareness

Phonological awareness is a metacognitive skill, which means having the ability and skill to recognise that words are formed by smaller units of sound called Phonemes.

Through manipulating and changing phonemes one can generate new words and meanings. Phonological awareness includes speech sounds, syllables, and rhymes. Phonics is the mapping of speech sounds (phonemes) to letters or letter patterns (graphemes)

When an individual has poor phonological awareness, they may find it difficult or struggle to answer the following types of questions.

- List all the words you can think of that rhyme with the word "Look "?

- Think of a word you could make if you were to change the "s" sound in the word "seed"to a "w" sound.

Phonics however builds upon the base of phonological awareness; when individuals learn to spell and read, they develop and hone their knowledge of the relationship between phonemes and graphemes within written language. However, a dyslexic person may often struggle with understanding these relationships within language.

PART 2

BEFORE KNOWING

CHAPTER 3

EARLY EDUCATION

Pre-School

As a small, pre-school child my development and early learning was quite normal. I began to walk when I was eleven months old, and as I understand it, I was one of those babies who did not crawl; I found it more fun to roll around the floor to get to my destination.

Gradually as I found that I could use my legs to get about, I wanted to explore more and more, and that made life extremely exciting for me. At the same time, it brought anxieties for my parents, because I was getting into places that I shouldn't.

Nursery School

Time passed so quickly because there was so much to do and see and before long, the day arrived for me to start Nursery School. It was a small, private school. I had a uniform and that made me feel very grown up.

The first day came and off I went with my parents in the car. When we got to the gate, suddenly I was not quite so sure that I wanted to go, but in I went.

There were two ladies who met me, a young teacher and a lady much older. They said to my Mum,

"El will be alright, leave her with us now."

With that my mum left.

I remember crying and trying to go after Mum, but it was no good, she had left me with people I didn't even know, and I didn't like it one little bit.

The older lady, who was exceedingly kind (just like my grandmother) and picked me up and tried to console me. When I eventually quietened down, she took me to play with the toys and to meet the other children. I soon settled in and began to enjoy their company. I made special friends with a little girl named Elizabeth and we remained friends throughout the time I lived in Kettering.

There were all kinds of games and puzzles to help us to learn different skills, and still no problems showed. By then I was happy in Nursery School and loved exploring new ideas with the various games and toys available. The story times were always fun as well. Perhaps the fact that the older lady always told us stories, and that I liked her, made it special for me.

Primary School

When I had just turned four years of age, I began school like everyone else from the group in the infants' first class. I grew and developed because we stayed at school all day. I liked school and enjoyed the different lessons.

Letter Confusion

As we began to do more writing, I was found to be confusing various letters - b and d, p and q in particular - and many other letters I would form backwards. In the beginning no-one paid much attention to that, after all many children do that kind of thing at age four and five.

I was about six and a half years old when my teachers said to my parents,

"El can do so much better in school if only she would concentrate more. She is very quiet and good, but she does not get on with her work."

Forgetting

Time passed and perhaps the teacher would read us a story. I loved stories and I would listen, but when the teacher would ask questions to encourage us to re-tell the story, I just didn't respond, I couldn't, because I didn't remember large parts of the story. This happened time and time again, and the teacher seemed to ask me more and more questions, and I couldn't answer. I was beginning to get frightened when it was story-time, knowing that the teacher was going to ask me questions that I wouldn't be able to answer. I did not understand why others knew the parts that I couldn't remember having been read.

The teacher was sure that I was being naughty and not bothering, and I could not understand why she was getting cross with me. All this began to make me feel very unhappy. So much so that I began to cry when it was time to go to school each morning. When asked what was wrong by Mum and Dad I could not answer; I did not realise what was happening.

Not only was writing rather a problem, I was also slow doing it and hardly ever managed to get all the work done that the others did. When there was reading, I could recognise the letters quite well, but stringing them together to make words was another matter. They were never in the right order; usually all the right letters were there but they were jumbled up. Getting them right was an extremely slow process.

My teacher became more and more convinced than ever that I was one of those children who either didn't want to work or couldn't work. At the same time, I found myself liking her less and less, I suppose because of her attitude towards me.

Despite the problems, I had a really good sense of humour. During the school holidays, I bought a small furry mouse. It looked quite life-like, and I teased lots of people with it. So, after the holidays, on the first day back, I took it to school with me and just for fun, I left it on the teacher's seat. Well, that was the worst thing I could have done. She was furious! When she asked who the mouse belonged to, naturally I said that it was mine, but oh dear, things went from bad to worse. Not only was I the 'problem child' to her, but also the one who played jokes on her too. She simply had no time for me from then on and at times she was very unkind and would often show me up in front of the class, and that hurt me so much.

Eventually my parents decided that enough was enough. They took me away from the school and sent me to another school in the town.

By this time, I was six years old; a little girl who was unhappy about school. Although deep down I wanted to go to school, the experiences were distressing me.

New School

It was September 1981, and a fresh school year was about to commence and for me that meant my first day at a new school. I wondered if the new teachers there would be kind and helpful.

Fortunately, during the holidays, quite by accident I had met two girls who already went to what was to be my new school. They were twin sisters, Kate and Judith, so at least I knew someone.

Kate and Judith were waiting for me on my first morning; they really helped me to settle in quickly. I soon got to know the other children and made new friends.

The Headmistress had been told about my difficulties at my previous school and had said just enough to my new teacher, so that she would understand if I was not settling too easily. She was so kind, which was such a contrast to my previous teacher. At last, I began to relax a little and talk more freely. But my learning difficulties were still there. It became increasingly obvious that my problems were not caused by emotional upsets, but there was rather more to it than that.

When various teachers spoke to my parents, they were still inclined to say things like,

"I do wish you would plug EI in before she comes to school; she is so sensible, she obviously has the ability to do much more, but she just will not concentrate."

It was the same old story. Mum and Dad tried to encourage me at home. I was telling them I was doing my best, but nothing was really working. I was getting cross and irritable again, and the frustration of my forgetfulness was terrible at times.

In fact, it was beginning to have an effect on us all.

Time went by and one day I had a little test, but my answers could not be read, that was until my teacher put the paper in front of a mirror, and surprise, surprise, it became readable! Real 'mirror writing' without even trying! More and more I confused certain letters like b and d, p and q, and still my teachers would tell my parents the same thing,

"El has the ability to do much better, but she does not concentrate, and she is so slow doing her work."

By this time, I was nearly eight year's old and was falling further behind with my work. My parents were getting a little concerned because I was not achieving as my teachers' thought I should, and to add to the problem I was getting frustrated.

At home Mum was beginning to notice that when she asked me to do something, I often went off to do it but never did the task. Whenever Mum asked when I was going to do it, my reply was always.

"Oh, I had forgotten."

You know how mums are; she just thought I did not want to do it, so I conveniently forgot, well that was not quite right – the fact is that I really did not remember.

The same kind of thing would and still does happen. I would be asked to fetch something and off I would go, but back I would come because I could not remember what I had gone for - more frustration for me and exasperation for Mum.

It was because of these problems that Mum, and Dad decided to seek help to find out whether there was a reason for my forgetfulness and poor schoolwork.

CHAPTER 4

SEEKING ADVICE

My mum, who had read about children with learning difficulties, then decided to write to the *Institute for Dyslexia*. She briefly explained my situation and in return they sent a questionnaire for my parents to fill in. This they did and as a result, an appointment was made for me to go to the *Institute for Dyslexia Assessment Centre* in Lincoln for an assessment just before my 8th birthday.

My parents felt that they should tell my Headmistress of their decision, as she was not at all sure they were doing the right thing. The Headmistress said that she was concerned that the experience of going there would upset me further. She also didn't think I was old enough to tell me why they were taking me. However, my parents still felt that they needed to know what was wrong in order to best help.

Mum and Dad explained that by going to Lincoln and doing the tests for the assessment, they would find out the reason why I was not able to remember as I should, and why I was unable to concentrate very well. It would then be possible to help me more.

Dyslexia Assessment and Diagnosis

It was a lovely sunny morning at the beginning of June when we set off in the car for Lincoln. The journey took about two and a half hours. Just before we reached Lincoln we stopped for lunch, and then went on for my two o'clock appointment.

I well remember that I didn't have much to say that morning. I was too preoccupied with wondering what was going to happen.

At exactly 2 pm, a lady came to the waiting room where we were sitting; she introduced herself and then took me upstairs to her office.

I had no idea what was going to happen. The lady had told my parents that the assessment tests would take about three hours. At eight years of age that length of time didn't register. But afterwards my parents said that it seemed forever and that they felt so helpless and kept thinking all kinds of thoughts about what my Headmistress had said and that I shouldn't be put through the ordeal.

Ordeal, yes it was! To begin with, the afternoon was hot, the lady was smoking almost the whole of the time, and I had a heavy bout of hay-fever … plus the tests. What an afternoon, and to top it all I was all alone with someone I didn't know.

The tests were varied, from having to solve problems, to repeating strings of numbers; you name it, I probably had to do it.

Eventually they did come to an end, and I was so glad to see Mum and Dad again. However, it wasn't quite time to go home as the lady wanted to talk to my parents for a while. I sat in another office drawing a picture while they conversed in the next room.

Results of the Tests

I could hear voices in the room next door, but I had no idea what was being said. I even tried to listen, but the walls were too thick. It was, after all, an old house that had been converted into offices.

The lady explained what the assessment tests had involved and how well or not I had responded. She then went on to say that she would be sending a full report to our home within ten days.

At last, I was re-united with my parents; we all thanked the lady for her time and help and then said good-bye.

The relief that we felt walking back to the car was tremendous. It was like walking on air. At least we were going home. We jumped into the car and made our way out of Lincoln as quickly as possible. In no time at all were pulling up at a restaurant for a much-needed snack and drink. How we all enjoyed it now that we could relax at last.

Refreshed, we got back into the car and headed for home. As we were nearing Kettering the sun was sinking, and the evening sky looked lovely as we sped through the countryside. It suddenly seemed hard to believe that so much had happened in one day.

That one day was about to make a considerable difference to my school life, although at the time I didn't know it.

The following morning, I went back to school and everything went on as before. Then about ten days later, as we had been informed whilst at Lincoln, the postman knocked on our door and handed Dad a large brown envelope. It was the detailed results of my assessment tests. There were pages of comments and it took some time for my parents to read and digest the contents.

The conclusions were that I had a short-term Auditory Retentional Difficulty, which, as I explained in the Introduction meant that I had a problem with remembering the spoken word in the short-term.

I could often recall what had been said hours or even days afterwards, but not immediately at the time it was said. Apparently, this condition was particularly severe according to the test results (although I was not told that at the time). The report went on to say that with specialised help, preferably on a one-to-one basis, then I might well learn to cope better with my poor memory and so improve my schoolwork. The assessment report emphasised that it would be a long, slow process and that my parents should not expect great results academically for me.

Certainly, the report had given some insight into the reasons for my lack of concentration and forgetfulness.

It left my parents' feeling concerned and wondering how much help would be available in my school. After all, the school I attended did not have the kind of resources for me to have continual support.

Despite this news, Mum and Dad went to see the Headmistress; before going they had given her the report to read. She was very sympathetic and said that now that the problem had been diagnosed, she would see that everything possible would be done to help me.

My parents were encouraged by what she said. Not only was she going to help as best as she could, she also informed them that there was a supply teacher who regularly came to school who had some limited training in helping children with specific learning difficulties (now referred to in education as Special Educational Needs (SEN).

My Headmistress arranged for the supply teacher to come to school for several lessons a week, and at the same time made the situation known to my class teacher.

CHAPTER 5

COPING WITH NEW WAYS OF LEARNING

The first thing the teacher did to help me with my dyslexia was to re-arrange our classroom so that it was possible for me to sit near to her, without it being obvious to the rest of the class. In this way she was able to keep checking that I had understood and remembered what was being said.

She was so kind and considerate. All of this was such a help, and the fact that she did not let the others know that I was having problems meant so much to me. The thought of being teased really frightened me. Nobody can truly understand or realise what you feel when you are made to feel different to your friends, unless you have actually experienced it for yourself.

This was a beginning; at last people were trying to understand and help.

At the same time the teacher with special training skills started visiting the school. Although this meant that I had to go out of normal class for the lessons, I didn't feel isolated because the Headmistress arranged that several others who needed extra help should also join me. This was a good thing for me and for them as well.

So, the process began, helping me to learn to spell better and recognise words more easily and thus improve my reading skills. Everything seemed to be going well, and slowly the teacher began to see some slight results. It was encouraging for all of us.

Then, after just one term, because of my dad's work we were going to have to move to a new house. It meant leaving the school and the teachers' who were trying so hard to help me and going to a new school in Plymouth. I didn't like the idea at all, and my parents knew that. They were rather concerned, but to Plymouth we went.

I was taken to visit what was to be my new school, and I had the opportunity to meet the person who was going to be my new Head Teacher. It was a gentleman this time.

When my parents explained the situation, he said that he was sure that the teachers' in his school would be helpful and understanding. After this, I was taken to see my new classroom and the teacher and children. I hoped I would soon make friends. The teacher introduced me to a girl named Hannah, who lived in the same street as me and that was encouraging. We said good-bye just until the following Monday morning, but before then we had to go into the city to buy my new uniform, which was grey and royal blue this time.

It didn't take me long to settle in and make new friends. Although I must admit I did miss my old friends and my previous school at times.

Shortly after my arrival at the school another new girl joined us named Kate, and within a few weeks she had moved into the house opposite to us. That was great as we got on well together right from the start. I think the fact that we were both new had something to do with it. We remained good friends throughout her time in Plymouth, and even though we both moved away from the area, we would still write occasionally and keep in touch.

Somehow though, my work progress was not very satisfactory. At first my teacher felt that it was probably due to the move.

Time passed and eventually my parents found themselves back in the Head Teacher's office to discuss the matter. My Head Teacher said that he personally couldn't recall having had to ever deal with a problem of this nature. He suggested that my parents' consider applying for a place for me to receive special help, which could be on a half-day release each week from school at the Mannamead Centre.

Mannamead Centre

He further explained that some parents wouldn't consider it because they felt it labelled their children as failures. After much discussion, my mum and dad felt that if there was help to be had, then it was worth a try.

An application was made for a place for me and then we had to wait several weeks for a reply. In due course a letter arrived from the Educational Authority inviting my parents and myself to a special morning session at the Centre to find out more about the aims and how it worked.

There were about twenty other children and their parents present. We, the children, were taken to a room next door to where our parents were. If I remember correctly, we were allowed to draw a picture, read, or play with one of the games available, and of course get to know the other children.

All our parents then settled down to listen to what the lady in charge had to tell them about the teaching procedures. They were told right from the beginning that their children would only get something out of it if the parents' were also prepared to work for about an hour every evening with us, doing whatever we had been assigned for the week. In fact, no child was accepted onto the scheme unless one parent or guardian was prepared to go to the session with their child. It needed real commitment.

It was also stressed that some children would get on and succeed much better and quicker than others. Each child would be encouraged to work at his or her own speed. It was also explained that accuracy and ability to retain each assignment was an important thing. The picture that was painted was not particularly attractive, but there was hope, real hope, that each child could just potentially become a success story. Let's be honest, every little thing learned and retained is a step towards greater success.

Spelling

Before we left, we all were allowed to choose three books from the Centre's library to read or have read to us during the summer holidays. We also each had a sheet of basic words, about one hundred in all, and we had to see how many of them we could learn to spell by the time when we started at the Centre in September.

The school holidays passed all too quickly, and all too soon it was September and time to go back to school. I went to my new class at Primary School and each Thursday morning I was released to attend Mannamead Centre.

When the first day came for me to go to my first lesson, Mum and I went in the car; it only took about five minutes from our house to the Centre. We arrived in good time and found that there were three other children there for the Thursday session, each with their mum. The morning was quite informal, and we soon got to know each other and discovered that we were all much the same age.

We were tested in turn for spelling. This was not in front of each other, but carried out on a one-to-one basis, so nobody was made to feel better or inferior to anyone else. When our abilities had been assessed, we were then given our individual assignments for the morning and for the following week.

Each week I would have some spelling to learn; to begin with never more than five or six words each week. In order to learn them, I had to write out the words lots of times, one at a time, until I found that I could write them without looking at them. I thought it was really boring, and hated it, but I did it and it was a method that worked for me. I also used cards with the words on to help me learn to recognise them. As time went by, I was encouraged to put each word into a sentence that made sense.

Reading Practise

Reading was particularly troublesome for me, so I had to do some reading practice on a daily basis. The idea was to encourage me to read aloud, and that was something I didn't like doing at all. Each evening Mum would sit with me and read a story that I had chosen. The idea being that if it was a story that I liked, then I would probably be motivated to try to read some of it myself; especially if I had chosen the story because I was familiar with it, then I would feel more able to read.

Mum would always be the one to start unless I said that I wanted to do so. Invariably as the story proceeded, I would feel that I wanted to take part. Perhaps this all sounds silly, but for someone with little or no confidence it is a method that does help to build up self-confidence in reading. Reading has never been easy for me: my memory goes blank on the easiest of words sometimes, and then it sounds as though I simply can't read properly.

I have been teased so much, that I just hate reading in front of people even now, but I know in my heart of hearts that I CAN READ, even though others may poke fun.

The homework from Mannamead got quite heavy as time went on; it was so time- consuming and I often got very frustrated at not being able to remember words and spellings, that possibly only the day previously I had got right. There were times when I got so mad that I would throw the books across the table and then burst into tears. I would even storm out of the room. Many a time I felt like giving up and not bothering, but Mum and Dad would patiently point out the improvements that were taking place and encourage me to not give in.

During this time, I was also having my daily school homework to contend with as well. So, it meant twice as much for me as anyone else, and at that time it didn't seem at all fair to me.

Teasing

School was going on much as usual, but it did seem that, at times people considered that because I went to

Mannamead each week, my help could be left to the Centre's teaching. In other cases, I am sure some people just thought I was not capable of doing my work. It was extremely hurtful at times. Just because someone cannot put their ideas onto paper in a sensible manner, doesn't mean that they are stupid or unable to learn.

If you are experiencing such hurtful teasing, try to ignore it. It's not easy I know but remember that most people do not understand your problem; if they did, they would certainly not say things that hurt you. But whatever you do, don't ever give up because the struggle will all be worth it in the long run - and make sure that your parents or carers don't let you give up either.

Time went by and it was good to know that I was not alone as many other children also had learning difficulties, and all were going through similar struggles and feelings as myself.

Speaking Ideas – Dictaphone / Tape Recorder

About two months before the final term at Mannamead, the lady who was in charge had to make recommendations for possible help within the classroom situation. Among her recommendations was that I be permitted to speak my ideas into a personal tape-recorder

(Dictaphone) when writing an essay, so that I would be able to refer to it in the course of my writing. The idea was good, quite helpful. I used the idea at home, but it was considered that it would be disruptive for others in the class if I be allowed to use the method there, so that was a non-starter as far as school was concerned. She also suggested that I continue to sit near to the teacher, in order that my confidence could be built up further. Mannamead had done so much to boost my self-confidence.

Statement !

It was then suggested that my parents allow the school authorities to have me 'statemented.' Again, Mum and Dad were reminded that many parents would not permit 'statementing" because they felt that there was a stigma attached to such. My parents view was that if it meant that it would ensure that I received the help required for the period of time that it was needed, then it had to be good in the long run.

So it was that I was 'statemented.' This meant that I had to have a medical examination, including sight and hearing tests.

The hearing test results initially revealed me to be a child who was profoundly deaf; that is until the doctor whispered something to me, and surprisingly I heard and answered. The doctor's conclusion was that my hearing was fine, but that I might be experiencing difficulty with hearing high-pitched sounds. Years later in a science lesson (physics) I found out this was true; when a teacher played different pitched noises through a speaker and asked the class to put up their hands when they ceased to hear the noise, I put my hand up before the rest of my classmates, because I couldn't hear the frequency the rest of my classmates could.

The sight test was done at school and nothing was found to be amiss, although since the age of six years old I had complained about the print in books going blurred. The response of all the opticians to this was that I was a little girl who just wanted to wear glasses. In their opinion, there was nothing wrong with my eyesight. But I will share more about that later.

The reports from the various sources, including school doctors' and school psychologist were gathered together, and as a result it was decided that I needed special help in view of my poor memory. This meant that a teacher would need to be available in a normal classroom situation to help me as required.

As my year at Mannamead Centre ended, I was sorry that I might not see the others in my group very often from then on, as we all attended different schools. We said our goodbyes. It was sad also having to say good-bye to the lady teacher who had done so much to help us during the year. She really was a dedicated and understanding person. Every school should have such a teacher to help those pupils with special needs. I never ever saw or heard her get cross, she was simply great.

School holidays were upon us once more, but as usual the time went by quickly. Before long, it was time to return to school for my final year in Primary School. It proved to be a fairly uneventful twelve months. I plodded on with my work, but at least there was someone extra in the classroom for some of the time. I was getting a little more attention, which helped of course. During that year we were preparing to go on to a new comprehensive school, which held lots of excitement and anticipation, together with some anxiety.

It was also during that year that I began learning to play the flute. This was a great confidence booster, as I got on really well with it. Indeed, I still, continue with my study of it and really enjoy playing the flute. Creativity is a great outlet for dyslexics, and often one that they are gifted in. Creativity is an excellent was way for dyslexics to build confidence and self-esteem. For me creativity came in the form of learning different musical instruments (flute, piccolo, guitar, and drums) along with cooking and various arts, crafts and DIY projects in the years that lay ahead.

PART 3

COMPREHENSIVE SCHOOL AND GCSEs

CHAPTER 6

STARTING COMPREHENSIVE SCHOOL

When places were allocated, I did not get my first choice of Comprehensive School, simply because I happened to live on the wrong side of the road. This meant that all my friends - those who understood a little of my difficulties and did not make me feel different - would go to one school and me to another. To begin with that thought really upset me.

The school authorities gave my parents a choice of three other schools, two of which were more than five miles away. Mum and Dad set about making appointments to visit the schools concerned, to see what they had to offer and how they would react to my difficulties.

One afternoon my parents went to see one of the schools, which was five miles away from our home. They received a very warm welcome from the Headmaster who proved to be more than helpful and sympathetic to their questions about the school, and how they would respond to having me as a pupil. In fact, they were so impressed that they decided that this was the school for me.

Just before the end of the summer term, I went to an open day at what was going to be my new school. I was rather nervous going in that morning, as I did not know anyone else who was going. At least that was what I thought. I had a big surprise when I got there, because one of the girls who I had been with at the Mannamead Centre was there as well.

I immediately felt more relaxed. It proved to be a very interesting and informative day. I enjoyed it so much that I was sorry when it came to an end. From then on, I could not wait to start my new school.

Starting Comprehensive School

During the summer we went out and purchased my new uniform. All the colours were quite different, so it made a nice change.

Eventually, the first day of term dawned. On with my new uniform and suddenly I felt very grown-up, but at the same time everything was new, and I was a bit apprehensive although deep down, I was looking forward to it. My new Comprehensive School was much larger than my previous school, with over a thousand pupils, in contrast to four hundred in my Primary School.

As the buses were not very convenient from my home to school, I was fortunate that Mum and Dad acted as my chauffeur each day. As we drove to school, I wondered if my new teachers would understand me. Would they be helpful? Would I be shown up in front of the rest of the class? But I needn't have worried because everyone seemed to be aware of my situation, and there was an extra teacher on hand for the lessons as and when she might be needed.

However, there were some minor hitches such as the fact that I was put in a special group for English. It was so basic that I felt as if I was back at Mannamead, which really made me feel low. Mum went to discuss the matter with my head of year, and I was later put into a mixed ability group and that helped to restore my confidence for a while.

However, as time went by, my teacher proved to be less and less sympathetic and helpful, even to the point of reducing me to tears on many occasions. In retrospect, I feel that the teacher simply didn't understand my problem, or had no time for those who were not producing 'A' grade work. My English went down during the course of the first year.

Maths also proved to be a stumbling block. Again, I was assigned to the lowest group, although I was getting my work right and finding it particularly boring because it was too easy. It was considered that if it was easy, I would get it done quickly and prove that I was ready to go on to more complex and difficult work. But for me, the boredom of the work just caused me to switch off and not get on with it. No matter what I said, it did not help. The rest of the subjects were not bad, and I was placed in mixed ability groups. My only problem was, not having sufficient time to get the class work done.

I was enjoying the new subjects, except for French, which I was not particularly good at. In fact, I found it especially difficult. I was happy doing Science subjects and loved Art, and the CDT (Craft, Design and Technology) subjects. My first report proved quite good on the whole, excluding English and Maths. Music was a special pleasure. I joined the school orchestra and had lots of opportunities to do extra playing, which led to school concerts. I even joined with the school orchestra on visits to other schools to give special concerts. I loved it.

At this point, I must refer back to my eye-sight tests that I had had, because of being 'statemented.'

By the middle of the first year of Comprehensive School, I was complaining of having difficulty keeping the print in focus. It kept going blurred. After much quizzing by my mum, I was taken to an optician again. Upon examination he found nothing wrong, but Mum explained and persisted that she felt something was not right. Eventually he wrote a letter to our doctor. In due course we made an appointment to see the GP and my mum explained the situation to him, and as a result he got an appointment for me at the Eye Infirmary in Plymouth.

Convergence

The consultant asked both Mum and me lots of questions, and then set about examining my eyes. Her diagnosis was that I was slightly short-sighted, but my real problem was one of "convergence." In a normal situation, a person can bring their eyes to focus on an object or dot within a few centimetres of the tip of the nose. But for me, I could not hold things in focus at 18 inches away. At long last the source of the trouble had been identified, and with the help of the Ophthalmologist and regular exercises things improved.

Obviously, it was going to take longer to see some improvement because the problem had gone undiagnosed for so long. Not only was I started on exercises straight away, but I was also prescribed bi-focal spectacles for schoolwork. These helped me enormously. Wearing them meant that the print no longer blurred, and I continued to wear my normal glasses for schoolwork.

The second year meant pupils were being streamed for English and down I went to a much lower group again, although not the very basic group. My first year (Year 7) teacher had almost written me off for English, having said to my parents that I simply did not have the ability. I was, in that particular teacher's opinion, a very low ability child. Thank goodness though, my parents' kept encouraging me and so set about trying to restore my self-esteem.

As I progressed through the second year (Year 8), my new teacher proved much more approachable and gradually my work began to improve. She noticed that with encouragement I was beginning to respond positively again and, by the end of the second year, my English had improved considerably. I was starting to write essays, although they were perhaps rather shorter than would normally be expected, but I was getting there slowly.

My difficulty when writing an essay was, and still is to some extent, the fact that I think of something that I want to say, but as I am writing it down, I lose my train of thought. So, I have to go back to the beginning and start thinking all over again.

At home, I would tell my mum my ideas and then dictate to her what I wanted to say and by doing it that way, I didn't have to think and write at the same time. To do two things at once in the early days was particularly difficult; not only was I trying to think about my story line but also think of how I was going to spell the words as I wrote them down and, oh dear, I would go blank in the process and have a complete mental block. It still happens nowadays but not as often, because although my spelling is not great, it is better than it used to be. My teachers' might well wonder how much my spelling has really improved today, given how it used to be!

The second year brought no real increase in the maths output per lesson. I simply turned off due to the simplistic nature of the mathematics. On the other hand, my other subjects were quite reasonable. The main complaint that I used to hear was,

"El works well, but she is too slow with her work. What she does is good, but there isn't enough done."

On the other hand, my art teacher was pleased with me, even to the point of praising my work. Similarly, my music teacher was also very encouraging, as were the teachers' for my CDT subjects, so it wasn't all gloom.

With that overall feedback I moved on into my third year. I was just thirteen years old, but this would be a year which was going to be quite important and strategic to my future, as I would be selecting which subjects I would choose for my options.

At the beginning of the school year, I did not really have much in the way of ideas of what I might eventually like to do as a career. This bothered me to begin with, as most of my friends had at least some thoughts about what they wanted to be and do.

I waited and as time passed, the art teacher mentioned that he hoped that I would consider Art as an option, because he felt that potentially a career in that line might be a good and viable path for me to consider. I loved art but I did not think such a career was for me. Nonetheless it was great to be affirmed in my artistic talent as it was something in which I excelled. My Home Economics teacher also felt that I had potential in that particular subject, and my Music teacher said that she hoped I would consider music as a possible option too.

I was so encouraged that some of my teachers were being so affirmative and positive to me about these possible options. But I was frustrated and a bit disappointed about important subjects such as English, Maths and Sciences - they were another story.

My teachers of these topics did not think it would be possible for me to be able to take English GCSE level. I would have to take a lower examination. Unfortunately, the expected outcome for maths was the same. They did not think I would be able to cope with Maths at GCSE level.

Although I loved science lessons and had a keen interest in it, still my teachers did not think I had much hope of achieving good exam results. They woefully declared,

"She simply doesn't get enough done, especially under exam conditions."

All of this was said and made known to me at the beginning of 1989. I knew then that I would not be able to take both Art and Music. The school curriculum in Plymouth would not allow me to take both, because I also had to take the three science subjects. Things were not looking good for me!

My parents' had been considering a move to North Wales for some months, but they were waiting to hear that they could definitely have the property they wanted. At last, the news came that they had secured the house, and we were once again on the move. Of course, I had mixed feelings about moving and having to make new friends and get used to a new school, especially now I was about to start on my GCSE's.

We moved north, and I was taken to meet my prospective Head of Upper School. Again, my situation had to be explained, as well as a full report being forwarded on from my former school. I was accepted into school, pending a final decision by the school psychologist.

The gentleman read the reports from my previous school and agreed that I could attend the new school. Furthermore, he felt that 'statementing' should no longer stand, and instead my teachers' should be made aware of my dyslexia and the challenges it presented me with. This was all tremendous news and the good news just kept on coming, as I was placed into a mixed ability English group and put up into a higher Maths group. I am glad to say that I was able to keep up and do the same work as the others.

CHAPTER 7

PREPARING FOR GCSEs

My options had to be decided upon almost as soon as I arrived here in my new school. I was advised to concentrate on my best subjects. My heart was torn at that point because I enjoyed science and had a keen interest in it but was better at other subjects, so in the end I dropped the science subjects in favour of CDT and was able to take both Art and Music. English also became a GCSE subject as did Maths. All this really helped me to settle down and restored my confidence so much. It made me feel glad that I had not given up in the past, when on many an occasion I was ready to, especially when in my frustration at not being able to remember what I had supposedly learnt, I would throw books across the table.

If you are a person who is encountering specific learning difficulties, let me say from my experience, do not ever give up! Keep plodding on, no matter how hard it may seem, because with help and encouragement from your parents' or guardians' there is much that you can achieve. It is quite surprising also how you learn to work around certain difficulties, especially the older you get.

I do sincerely hope that you too will also have the courage and that you will go on against all the problems and setbacks that you will encounter along the way.

To parents and carers, I would like to say, don't let your son or daughter give up, encourage him or her just like my parents' have encouraged me, and indeed still continue to do so. It's that kind of belief in me that my parents gave that made me believe that I could do the work.

GCSEs

During the lead up to and including my GCSE years at school, I was incredibly fortunate to have two inspirational teachers. These were Marina Hughes, who was my Catering / Home Economics / Technology teacher, and Val Evans, my English teacher. Marina and Val not only taught me those subjects, they taught me to believe in my own capabilities. They supported and built up my confidence, which was at an all-time low.

Marina Hughes inspired me to follow my passion for cooking. Catering and Art were the subjects I excelled at. My English teacher Val Evans transformed my English. She was so passionate and inspiring in lessons, as well as being encouraging. She helped me to believe I could get a good GCSE in English. You see at my previous school the English teacher had written me off because I was dyslexic, that I was "thick" and could not achieve. Looking back, it was due to her ignorance of the subject of dyslexia but at the time it was very hurtful and demoralising.

Study Methods and Aids

I am a visual and kinaesthetic learner, which means I tend to have a stronger visual and experiential memory. As a result, I tend to learn best via seeing and drawing diagrams and mind maps, and also by physically practicing the subject.

I found it was important to plan a revision timetable, so that I had sufficient time to cover all my subjects. In addition to this, I worked out what was the most effective and productive time for me to study. I encourage anyone with dyslexia to do the same. My most productive time was in the evenings, but others may find early mornings are better for them. I also found that if I planned my subject revision to incorporate a mix of subjects – some I found easy and others more difficult – this helped me to feel that I was achieving. Similarly, breaking my learning into bite-size goals was another helpful method I used to assist me in my revision to see that I was achieving and making progress.

At the end of the day, each individual should use whatever methods works best for them, whether it be flash cards, diagrams, mind maps, reading, listening to audio revision, or getting involved with interactive revision sessions.

For my exams I was granted 25% extra time which was of great assistance because I had a Short-Term Memory problem, which meant that I needed to read and re-read questions significantly more that the average pupil to remember and comprehend what the question was asking of me, so the additional time allowed for this and enabled me to complete my exams.

While taking exams I also found the most effective way for me to complete them was to do the easier and quicker questions first, and then tackle longer and more involved questions after those.

Help Available

There is various help available for taking exams and assessments within schools and colleges. This additional assistance can be applied for via the educational establishment you* or your child is attending (*if you are an adult learner). Please see Appendix 4 for a list of organisations that can assist you in this regard.

Extra Time

The amount of extra time for exams and assessments can vary dependent on the individual student's needs. It can incorporate additional help such as:

Reader

This is where a pupil has someone to read the questions aloud to them, which may help when a pupil is a slow reader or comprehends more effectively if they hear rather than read information.

Scribe

This is where a pupil has someone to write down their answers in the form of dictation. A scribe must write the answer exactly as it is dictated to them, so that it gives a true representation of the pupil's understanding of the question. This helps pupils who struggle with writing (such as extremely poor handwriting or ability to get what they want to say down on paper).

Use of Information Technology

The use of information technology_such as computers, laptops or tablets (IT) is very helpful for pupils who have difficulty with handwriting and spelling.

Calculators

Calculators can be used for additional help within mathematics where needed.

Overlays / Tinted Spectacles

The use of these aids greatly helps to reduce the written word on the page from being fuzzy, jumping around on the page, or the white page dazzling the reader. Coloured paper can also be of assistance in these circumstances.

PART 4

ADULTHOOD EXPERIENCES OF DYSLEXIA

CHAPTER 8

EARLY CAREER PATH

After my GCSEs, I applied for a job as a trainee Dental Nurse. For the first couple of months, I thoroughly enjoyed my work. I found it interesting, and it was building my self-confidence.

In the September of that same year, I applied to college to study Dental Nursing at night school, along with two years on-the-job training / chair-side experience.

I have always been interested in nature and human biology. I love to watch medical programs, and I am intrigued by how the human body works. The Dental

Nursing course was predominately head and neck biology, which I found fascinating.

The course included anatomy, identification and use of dental surgery tools and equipment, treatments, sterilisation, cross-contamination control, and administration.

I used a Dictaphone to aid with note taking and studied hard. The study tools I employed were flash cards with pictures of instruments and their uses. I even borrowed a skull from a dental colleague to help me learn the different bones and locations of nerves and their entry and exit points! I would ask the dentist I was working with about any questions that arose from the course, or anything I did not understand. The dentist I worked with was incredibly supportive and would ask me questions during the day to help consolidate my learning. This was so helpful.

The time for the exam duly came around. The exam involved oral and practical elements along with the written exams, which included identification of instruments and the practical use of them. I passed all except for the written exam. The first time I took the exam I wasn't given the extra time I needed because of my dyslexia, and I did indeed run out of time and failed to complete all the questions. My employer at the time said I should have passed because she thought I was an exceptional Dental Nurse.

The second time I was due to take the exam I fought for extra time and passed easily. Ultimately, I went on to train other dental nurses in various dental practices I worked in.

I remained a Dental Nurse for over ten years, after which I decided that I needed a fresh challenge and moved into a different line of work.

Do Not Allow Yourself to Be Written Off

I have found that in most seasons of my life there has been prejudice regarding my dyslexia. I have encountered people who have written me off, before even giving me a chance. Having said that, I am happy to observe that times are changing and there is now much more understanding out there than there used to be.

In my adult life I have tended to hide my dyslexia as much as possible, especially in the first instance, so that I can at least have a chance to prove my abilities without being subjected to prejudice, ignorance or lack of understanding regarding how dyslexia may or may not affect me.

As a dyslexic I have learnt ways around a lot of my dyslexic traits. For example, lists have become my friends at home and at work, because of my short-term auditory retention difficulty. I will either ask someone to leave me a note or send an email etc. so that I can read it as many times as required in order that I can remember or comprehend the content or to confirm what a person has requested.

Computers are great in so many ways for a dyslexic; they help with formatting, presentation, spelling, grammar and also aid you to function at your true ability. In this way, technology helps to reveal a person's true capacities in multiple areas.

I believe it is imperative that schools, colleges, universities, and workplaces truly grasp that dyslexia is in no way about a person's intellectual ability. Rather than seeing it as a hindrance, it can be considered a gift of difference. Yes, there are certain aids that help a dyslexic along the way, however this is most importantly about unlocking their specific learning style and techniques, and facilitating them to reach their full potential.

Dyslexics are often highly intelligent, have an eye for detail and think very creatively due to having to learn ways around the challenges they may have experienced. In other words, they are an asset to the workplace and education establishments.

I believe that in education there needs to be more consistency in understanding dyslexia and how to unlock a dyslexic person's learning potential, while instilling self-confidence and self-belief in them.

In the workplace there needs to be a greater awareness of dyslexia. It *is not a disability* which affects intelligence or ability, and doesn't prevent the individual from being good at their work, or that in some way makes them to be less intelligent than the average person. The fact is, dyslexics are often highly intelligent and great problem solvers, and have excellent eye for detail.

I have been written off many times by prejudice and a lack of understanding. However, I learnt a long time ago not to allow myself to be defeated by others lack of knowledge about dyslexia. How did I accomplish this? By having a steadfast and genuine self-belief in what I can and cannot do, playing to my strengths and constantly developing areas of weaknesses.

The following are some different methods that can be used to cope with dyslexia:

- **Lists** – These help with planning and poor memory.

- **Written Notes** - Asking teachers and lecturers for written notes on lessons can take the pressure off dictation and note-taking within lessons.

- **Spelling and Grammar Check** - Spelling and grammar check facilities on PC's and tablets are a God-send for dyslexics because you do not have to worry about spelling things correctly. You can just focus on typing in the first instance and spell check later.

- **Reader Pens** – These can help improve your standard of reading and the speed at which you read. These pens are great for learning to read unfamiliar words, and for studying, especially if you experience reading fatigue. They will help you read text more quickly and assist with word recognition.

- **Screen Brightness Variation** - Varying the brightness on screens such as laptops, tablets and phones can help to eliminate, or at least ease, some of the vision disturbances you may experience as a dyslexic. Personally, I find this extremely helpful, as the brightness of the screen hurts my eyes and aggravates the fuzzy / moving letters.

- **Overlays / Colour Tinted Glasses** - Use overlays or colour tinted glasses if you find the glare of white paper too much, or the letters and words move around on the page. It is best to get a professional assessment for overlays or tinted glasses as this will help you to accurately discover which colour, or combination of colours, help with your vision.

- **'Blanks'** – When reading aloud in public or in groups I tend to get many blanks on even the simplest of words, for example – when, then, there, etc. I see the word; I know and recognise the word, but at the same time I can't get it from my brain to my mouth to verbalise it. So, I always opt to have the piece I need to read aloud prior to having to deliver it vocally. This helps me because I will then be familiar with the reading, and I am able to ad-lib if necessary or recite parts from memory. Prior reading helps to prevent staccato: stilted and disjointed flow of reading and facilitates more fluidity of reading.

- **Dictaphones** – I have found these are helpful in lecture and lesson situations, where you must take in a lot of information or make notes, as you can replay the recorded information as many times as necessary. Dictaphones are useful for revising as you can record the information you need to learn and listen to it, which can also take the pressure off reading a lot.

- **Audio books** – These are helpful for improving fluidity of reading if you use them along with the written text. Audio books can also help with the recognition and pronunciation of unfamiliar words.

CHAPTER 9

KNOW AND UNDERSTAND YOUR STRENGTHS

As a dyslexic it is important to know and understand your strengths, so that when you encounter obstacles, personal discouragement, or prejudice, you can stare it in the face, rise above it all and prove you can indeed succeed and achieve anything you put your mind to.

At school, my strengths were in Art, Catering, Craft Design and Technology.

My personality strengths are that I am honest, determined, ambitious, quiet, caring and a good listener.

My general strengths are that I am extremely practical, creative, artistic, and musical and I have a keen eye for detail.

When I assess and reflect on my strengths and weaknesses, I realise that I can think practically to make various DIY items and clothing without specific plans; I like to create items often from scratch. I enjoy practical problem solving. I am quite musical, playing various instruments (flute, piccolo, drums and guitar) and I enjoy being artistic and creative, making jewellery, greeting cards and whittling / carving wood – well to be honest, I will try anything crafty.

I recognise that a purely administrative office job would not be playing to my strengths, as the time restraints for sheer volume of paperwork might cause a little difficulty due to the need to read and reread documents because of my short-term memory difficulties. Also, personality wise, I don't mind some paper or administrative work, but I could not face sitting at a screen all day, as I like to be on the move.

Another aspect of work that would not play to my strengths is being a phone operative. Talking on the phone is not the most comfortable thing for me, because I must rely on my short-term memory, which as stated earlier is one aspect where dyslexia affects me.

Over time I have developed techniques to help me remember what is said during a phone call, often by making notes. These notes are trigger words or signs that spark my memory after the phone call, along with enabling me to gain key information in case I need to clarify different points that were discussed during the phone conversation. This isn't some magical system to remember, it is purely words or symbols that will trigger my memory; someone else looking at my initial notes may not understand them but the information that I need to remember and make specific notes for others are there for me to recall.

Unquenchable Thirst for Knowledge

As a child, I felt inadequate. I was usually the last to catch on to things at school due to my poor short-term memory. I felt I was on constant catch up and longed to be seen as capable and equal with my peers because I enjoyed learning new things, I just learnt in a different way.

I lacked confidence and was bullied frequently, ironically labelled as a swot, though the truth be known I was doing what I needed to do, to get by and try and keep up with my peers.

As a result, in adulthood I developed an unquenchable thirst for knowledge. This was partly due to feeling I had to prove myself adequate and capable, because I had to do this with the teachers at school who hadn't understood my dyslexia. I felt I needed to prove to them that I was intelligent and academically able, once I had found the learning techniques that unlocked my ability.

As I mentioned in Chapter 8, I left school and commenced training to become a Dental Nurse, which I found fascinating. I was lucky to work for a Dentist who saw my potential and noticed my interest in oral surgery and diagnosis of X-rays. She first taught me how to read the x-rays, pinpointing what might be causing a patient's problems. I thrived on learning about the various complexities of assisting with oral surgery and qualifying as a Dental Nurse.

My drive for knowledge continued to grow, and I went on to study Practical Theology; Contextual Theology; Biology, Anatomy and Physiology; Life Coaching; Clinical Weight Loss Coaching; Diet and Nutrition; Mindfulness, Counselling and Psychotherapy; Cognitive Behavioural Therapy and Massage Therapy. I guess you could say I am a perpetual student!

This goes to prove that all the teachers who wrote me off as a young person and said I would not even attain

GCSE's were wrong! This is why I believe it is so important to encourage dyslexics and help them unlock their learning potential. Too often people have assumed because I am dyslexic, I won't be able to complete a task or follow an instruction, that I must lack intelligence or academic ability but look at the overview of qualifications - I am intelligent and have gained many qualifications! This is living proof that dyslexics are intelligent and extremely capable!

To any dyslexics reading this – I want to say to you that I believe in you and I encourage you to keep persevering; you can achieve your full potential! Go for it!

CHAPTER 10

STARTING MY OWN BUSINESS

All through school and into adulthood, friends would come and talk to me about their problems and difficulties. I had a natural capacity to listen and empathise. Later on, when I experienced some personal difficulties in my own life through an extremely traumatic relationship, I decided to train as a counsellor (in Counselling and Psychotherapy). I realised that for some reason, people felt safe enough to share various things that were troubling them with me, and I wanted to be in a better position to help. I also wanted to assist people who have experienced similar difficulties to me, such as domestic abuse.

I studied hard and, implemented many of the techniques mentioned previously in this book. Along the way there were ups and downs; some things I found easy and others I found difficult, but I am delighted to say that after two years I passed my course in Counselling and Psychotherapy,

As time went on, I increased my knowledge, skill base and training to include Advanced Cognitive Behavioural Therapy, Mindfulness, Life Coaching and Massage Therapy. I had a vision to start my own business in Wellbeing Therapies, looking after the body, mind and wellbeing because so often our emotional health can affect the body and vice versa.

As anyone who has embarked on starting a business will know, it takes an immense amount of your time and energy. You need determination and perseverance, along with good organisational and administration skills to keep on top of all the various paperwork you need to process, not to mention all the skills and abilities you need to carry out your chosen profession.

Soon to be a Published Author

Not only have I written this book, I have also written another book about domestic abuse and my journey to freedom, which will soon be published. This is a book in which I share experiences as a domestic abuse victim, and how I left an abusive relationship and did indeed get stronger and am now living a life free from abuse.

Why do I Share This?

I am sharing this to show that it is possible to become a published author and have dyslexia.

If I had listened to the critics of my younger self, then I would not have amounted to much. I would have believed that I was stupid, slow or not academically inclined and would never have achieved all my qualifications or written two books.

For me, writing my books has not been an overnight process; it has taken an incredible amount of time and hard work, involving self-belief and determination along with a sense of being teachable during the various editing processes.

During the writing of these books, I also had to address the underlying feelings of inadequacy, because although I have accomplished so much, there are still times when I do not feel good enough due to comments from childhood years. When these feeling come to try and pull me down, I remind myself that I have achieved so much more than I or my critics ever thought possible. At these times I remember my inspirational teachers' Marina Hughes and Val Evans, who believed in me and instilled much of the confidence and recognition of my own potential to achieve anything I put my mind to.

All of which were spurred on, by the desire to bring awareness and understanding about Domestic Abuse and Dyslexia.

I passionately believe that dyslexia should not limit a person's aspirations or self-belief and should not be seen as a limiting factor in life, education or employment.

If anyone had told me as a child, that I would be the author of two books (so far), own a home, attain all these different qualifications and run a Wellbeing Therapy business, I would never have believed them. The old labels are slowly dissolving in the new identity of my personal development, success and achievements in education and in business.

As a result of this I am so passionate to instill encouragement, hope and belief in what dyslexic children and adults can ultimately achieve. With the right help and support, dyslexia should not hold anyone back from achieving their full potential, *if* they are taught the techniques that will help them overcome and conquer the challenges brought on by the condition

CONCLUSION

YOU CAN DO ANYTHING YOU PUT YOUR MIND TO

"You can do anything you put your mind to," was a phrase that my parents used to tell me constantly while growing up.

I found that phrase so frustrating at times because I was in the process of learning my various coping techniques for my dyslexia and it felt like an uphill slog.

With hindsight I have come to understand and believe it is so true - you can achieve anything you put your mind to. That is not to say that it will be easy, because inevitably there may be times when it is hard to achieve specific things. There will be ups and downs, successes and failures. However, the key is to never ever give up on your dreams, to keep on persevering and to have faith in your own knowledge and understanding of your strengths and abilities.

Quotes from Teachers and Work Colleagues

Former English Teacher – Mrs Val Evans

"I taught El Davies at YJB (Ysgol John Bright) during the latter part of El's lower school English and then during her GCSE years. When El arrived at YJB she was very quiet, shy and lacking in confidence. El's behaviour was good and attentive in class, always trying her best in what she did.

During El's time at YJB I saw her grow in confidence and ability with her English work.

El came from a school where she had been put in a low ability English class but we at YJB believed El was capable of so much more, so she was put into a mainstream English class where I saw El grow in ability and ultimately thriving and gaining good GCSE English results.

El had true determination to succeed. While El was my pupil she wrote a piece of work for her GCSE coursework about dyslexia. (which has formed the basis of this book many years later). I was so impressed with her understanding of dyslexia and how she overcame the obstacles it presented. The book she wrote for her English coursework was insightful, I showed it to the special needs coordinator Mrs. Hilda Jones who was also impressed with El's book. Hilda Jones felt that Professor Tim Miles may be interested in it and so we spoke to El about this. The result was that El sent her book to Professor Tim Miles at Bangor University's Dyslexia Unit. Professor Tim Miles wrote back after being so impressed with El's book he printed extracts in the Bangor University's Dyslexia Unit news bulletin and asked to keep a copy of the book on file for reference resource in the Dyslexia Unit. Professor Tim Miles also recommended the book for publishing along with giving El two publishing leads.

El was ecstatic to receive Professor Tim Miles letter with all the encouraging news. This was an enormous confidence booster for El. She has continued with her studies gaining many qualifications. El's thirsts for knowledge is unquenchable. I am delighted that El has gone on to achieve so much, she has truly NOT let dyslexia hold her back.

It is great to see El's interest in writing developing, this being the second book she has written and won't be the last! "

El is an inspiration for many pupils struggling with dyslexia, she has proved that with determination and hard work you truly can achieve amazing things! If El can do it…so can you!

Former Technology and Catering Teacher – Mrs. Marina Hughes

"It was a privilege and a pleasure to have known and taught El Davies. My role was as a Technology teacher. El did lower school Textiles and Catering in the upper school. She coped very well with both written and practical work. She impressed me with her sheer determination to succeed. Nothing was going to hold her back not even her dyslexia.

I have had the pleasure of following her continuing education and career since leaving my school and I am very impressed at the way she has progressed. She has *a thirst for learning, acquiring numerous qualifications and skills and now her writing. I am extremely proud of her".*

Chaplain & Colleague – Rev Nicky Lees

"El has shown amazing courage and determination despite all the problems she has experienced, especially Dyslexia. It is to her credit that her abiding focus has always been to encourage and support others".

Former Head of School & Colleague – Mr. G Flowers

"I found this book to be informative, inspiring and one I want to recommend to anyone who is interested in learning, education, child development, or people in general!

I worked with El for several years when she held the role of Lab Technician in a large Science Department in a secondary school. She struck me as a very calm, competent, and diligent colleague, always reliable in any situation. She was well prepared and had the confidence and respect of her teaching colleagues, who she would support patiently at all times. They came to work safe in the knowledge that their labs would be equipped with the correct equipment and chemicals at the right times.

This required the immense personal skills which El correctly identifies in the book, but also a sophisticated level of organisation and technical knowledge. The Sciences were popular A Level subjects and so required complicated demonstrations and experiments to be performed accurately, which in turn demanded a high level of expertise from El. Materials had to be ordered at the right times and health and safety regulations were paramount. El was able to keep on top of all facets of this varied role and must have used all of the techniques highlighted here to make such demanding work look so effortless.

This book is perfectly structured to inform someone new to this topic about all aspects of dyslexia. It is also detailed enough to deepen the knowledge of anyone experiencing dyslexia or supporting anyone who is, either in a professional or personal capacity.

At the heart of the book is the spirit of determination and enquiry embodied by El. I am sure everyone who reads this will come away feeling better informed, uplifted, and determined to help themselves and those around them overcome any obstacles to self-improvement.

I endorse this work whole-heartedly".

Head of Science & Chemistry, Colleague – Mr. P Lindberg

"It is to El's great credit that she shown the mental fortitude to overcome these barriers, but it still raises questions about why it was made so difficult".

"Within the science department, we often comment about how lucky we are to have such a talented, conscientious, and intelligent technician team, of which El is an integral part. The department has a strong reputation, both within school and in the wider community, and attracts the most A-level students each year. This is in no small part down to the efficiency, organisation, proactivity, and creativity displayed by El. By thinking through potential practical problems and solutions before they arise, she helps to improve the learning experience for the students and makes the teachers more effective".

Head of Biology & Colleague – Mr. P Armstrong

"Having worked with El for several years now, I have witnessed first-hand the benefit of her determined approach to life. She has not only written the advice in this book, but she lives it out every day.

As she remains acutely aware of her relative strengths and weaknesses, El consciously employs techniques to ensure her peak performance. In so doing, it turns out that she is much more reliable than an equivalent 'non-dyslexic' if they had a less reflective approach to their working life. Knowing that she is being purposely meticulous gives me the confidence to leave her to get on with any task and she takes great pleasure in a job well done. An environment of professional respect and friendly collaboration has allowed her to excel in tasks that ought not to play to her strengths, and I have been genuinely surprised at times with the quality of the written documents she has produced from her own initiative. We have also benefitted from her creative flair, where her blend of talents gives her the edge in the often-needed thinking outside the box.

In the department where El now works, she is held in high regard and appreciated greatly. My only hope is that this will contribute to her enjoying many years of fulfilling employment with us; something that she richly deserves".

I hope these quotes go a little way in encouraging you, the reader, that dyslexia does not have to hold you back, and that with hard work and determination you can succeed.

Keep working, never give up or give in. Believe in yourself and your abilities. You can do anything you put your mind too…If I can do it… so can you!

APPENDICES 1

Documentary: Education Manchester

Schoolboy Realises Dyslexia is a Superpower and Not a Disability

A while back there was a programme on television called Education Manchester. The then Head Teacher – Mr. Drew Povey - shared with a pupil struggling with dyslexia, how he too had coped with dyslexia and for 20 years had not told anyone at work that he had dyslexia. The pupil's reaction was total amazement that his "Head Teacher" could have dyslexia. Mr. Povey's reaction to the boy comments was "Why not! It's the best thing that happened to me because I think about things in a different way to other people".

This programme touched my heart, because I saw in the dyslexic boy's reaction a glimpse of inspiration: that if Mr. Povey could become a Head Teacher, then there was hope that he (the little boy) could also achieve success!

I recognised I had also experienced that same spark of self-belief and inspiration as that young boy, through my own teachers Mrs. Val Evans & Mrs. Marina Hughes.

The understanding of dyslexia from a personal view of the Head Teacher was clear, the acknowledgement that it would take time and a lot of hard work is so true, but the belief in that little boy was equally clear to see.

Teachers who create the sparks of self-belief in pupils - especially when pupils are struggling with Special Educational Needs such as dyslexics - really do make a difference and can inspire a pupil who has previously written off to achieve success in their life… I am living proof of that!

Thank you to all those inspirational teachers out there – you really do change the course of pupils' lives!

APPENDICES 2

VARK MODEL

Information about learning styles can be found in Educational theorist Neil Fleming's VARK model of Student learning.

VARK also known as the VAK model is an acronym which refers to the main four learning styles:

V -Visual

A – Auditory

R – Reading / Writing (preference)

K – Kinaesthetic

"Learning Styles again VARKing up the right tree!"

(Fleming & Baume 2006)

It is important to know that presenting the information needing to be learnt in a student's preferred learning style can greatly improve their learning and behaviour. It has been evidenced that giving a student this information in their preferred mode of learning, will increase a student's concentration, motivation, comprehension, and metacognition.

VARK Expanded information:

Visual Learners – prefer images, graphics, maps, diagrams, mind maps and video clips.

Aural Learners – prefer listening, speaking, for example lectures, and discussion groups. They will often use mnemonic devices and repetition as a study technique.

Reading / Writing Learners – prefer to learn through words, for example being avid readers and frequently making copious amounts of notes. They also have the ability to translate abstract concepts into essays, reports etc.

Kinaesthetic Learners – prefer learning though physical, experimental, practical, activities, role play and drama.

There are other learning styles, which are extension of the four main learning modes. These include: Verbal, Logical, Mathematical, Social and Interpersonal, and Solitary Intrapersonal learning.

APPENDICES 3

GLOSSARY AND USEFUL INFORMATION

Dyslexia – a specific learning difficulty that does not affect a person's intellect.

Learning Disability – Can impair the ability to learn and may also affect intelligence.

SEN (Special Educational Needs) – This is an umbrella term, which covers a wide range of specific needs such as behavioural, emotional and social difficulties; speech, language and communication; hearing and or visual impairment; multi-sensory impairment; autism, and physical disabilities.

SENCO (Special Educational Needs Co-ordinator) – SENCOs work to raise the educational achievements of pupils with special educational needs. SENCOs are experienced teachers with a passion for supporting SEN pupils. They lead and coordinate the provision and assistance that SEN pupils may require, helping them to get the most out of their education.

Special Needs Assessment – An appointment for the child and parents or guardians when the child is assessed to find out their specific special needs. This will take place prior to a statement being given, and this assessment will provide the information required prior to the statement.

Statement – Educational (Statemented Pupils) – This is a statement that sets out a child's needs and the help they should have. It is reviewed on a yearly basis to make sure all the child's needs are being met. An educational statement has six parts:

- General information about the child and the advice that was received from the Education Authority.

- A description of the child's needs after the assessment.

- What special help should be given to the child.

- Name and type of school the child should attend, and any arrangements out of school hours or off school premises.

- List of any non-educational needs the child may have.

- Ways in which the child will have the listed non-educational needs met.

Short Term Auditory Retentional Difficulty – Difficulty recalling the spoken word in short term but will most likely be able to remember the same spoken phrase / sentence etc. later for example in medium to long term.

Reader Pen / C-Pen / Exam Reader Pen – These are pen-like devices that will read written / printer text back to you. They can help in exams for slow readers, and these pens can also assist in improving reading though aiding the reader to recognise and pronounce the specific words.

Visual Distress – This is when a dyslexic has trouble with reading the written text due to seeing blurred, fuzzy, or moving letters / words on the page or screen. Also, visual distress can be experienced via a white page or screen appearing dazzlingly bright, which makes it hard to focus on the written text. Visual Distress can be alleviated using colour tinted acetate overlays or colour tinted glasses.

Colour Tinted Acetate Overlay – Reduces visual distress through reducing the glare from the written text on the page or screen.

Colour Tinted Spectacles - Reduces visual distress through reducing the glare from the written text on the page or screen.

Irlen Colour Assessment – This is the recommended assessment, which will identify the specific colour or combination of colours will help with a dyslexic's visual distress for tinted overlays. This assessment will ascertain which tint or combination of colour tints will be most effective for colour tinted glasses.

Dictaphone – Personal voice recorder,

Word Attack Skills – The ability to break down words in smaller words. for example identifying "sea" and "side" in the word "seaside."

Phonological Awareness – This is a metacognitive skill: the ability to recognise that words are formed by smaller units of sound called phonemes. Phonological awareness includes speech sounds, syllables, rhymes.

Phonemes – These are smaller units of sound, which are found in bigger words. Through manipulating and changing phonemes you can generate new words and meanings.

Phonics - This is the mapping of speech sounds (phonemes) to letters or letter patterns (graphemes). Phonics, however, builds upon the base of phonological awareness.

Graphemes – Are letter pattens

Visual Learners – Need to see the information in order to them help process it. Visual learners often use diagrams, charts, graphs, mind maps, pictures and other visual resources and medias to effectively and efficiently interpret and memorise the information they are trying to learn. The visual learning style is part of the Fleming VAK/VARK model,

Kinaesthetic Learners – Need to carry out physical / whole body movement to process new and difficult information. Cognitive skills are part of kinaesthetic, perceptual learning, and skill memory. Kinaesthetic learners acquire knowledge and new skill through hands-on practice and problem solving. In schools this type of learning may include role-play, dance, drama, races, projects, and field trips. This is also part of the Fleming VAK/VARK model.

VARK Model – ref to Neil Fleming Educational Theorist.

APPENDICES 4

USEFUL ADDRESSES

The British Dyslexia Association

Unit 6a Bracknell Beeches

Old Bracknell Lane

Bracknell

RG12 7BW

Tel: 0333 405 4555

Website: www.bda.org.uk

(Diagnostic Assessments for children and adults and workplace assessments, professional accreditation, training for individuals and organisations, free helpline for dyslexics, and those who support them i.e., friends, family, teachers and employers)

Dyslexia Institute UK

Tel: 07711070533

Email: dyslexiainstituteuk@gmail.com

Website: www.dyslexiainstituteuk.com

(Offering bespoke company training packages to ensure your company is "Dyslexia Confident")

Dyslexia Research Trust

179A Oxford Road

Reading

RG1 7UZ

Tel: 0118 958 5950

Email: info@dyslexic.org.uk

Website: www.dyslexic.org.uk

(Helps people with reading difficulties to achieve their full potential, through research, assessments, advice, services, raise awareness, influence policy makers to enable understanding and implementation of effective methods of remediation in schools, understand and champion the positive aspects of dyslexia.)

Mannamead Counselling

(Part of Optimus Dyslexia Assessment Services)

117 Mannamead Road,

Plymouth

Devon

PL3 5LL

Tel: 01752 269694

(Assessments for Dyslexia in adults and children, screenings for Dyslexia, Attention Deficit Hyperactivity Disorder, Autistic Spectrum conditions for adults and children, counselling, support groups for ADHD, and ASC which offer a mix of cognitive behavioural therapy, psychoeducation, mindfulness and mutual support)

Dyslexia Action (Head Office)

Centurion House

London Road

Staines-upon Thames

Staines

TW18 4AX

Website: www.dyslexiaaction.org.uk

Dyslexia Action Training Tel: 01784 222304

Dyslexia Action Shop Tel: 01784 222339

The Dyslexia Guild Tel 01784 222342

(Specialist teacher training, assessor training, dyslexia shop / resources)

APPENDICES 5

REFERENCE / INFORMATIVE BOOKS /REPORTS / PAPERS

Critchley, Macdonald. The Dyslexic Child, London William Heinemann 1970

Naidoo, Sandhya. Specific Dyslexia. Pittman 1972

Morgan, W.P (1896) A case of congenital word blindness, British Medical Journal

Hinshelwood, J (1917). Congenital word blindness. London: H.K. Lewis

Rose, J. (2009). Identifying and teaching children and young people with dyslexia and literacy difficulties. London: Department for Children, Schools and Families

Elliott, J.G. & Grigorenko, E.L. (2014). The dyslexia debate. New York: Cambridge University Press.

Miles, T.R. & Miles, E. (1999). Dyslexia: A hundred years on (2nd edn). Buckingham: Open University Press.

Elliott, J.G. & Grigorenko, E.L. (2014). The dyslexia debate. New York: Cambridge University Press.

AUTHOR BIOGRAPHY

El Davies may have dyslexia but has not let it define her. El is passionate about helping others to achieve their full potential, she believes better understanding, awareness and opportunities for dyslexics are vital for parents,' teachers,' employers' and, of course, dyslexic individuals.

El is trained in:

Counselling and Psychotherapy

Cognitive Behavioural Therapy

Life Coaching

Weight loss Coaching

Advanced Nutrition for Weight Loss

Mindfulness Teacher

Massage Therapy

National Dental Nursing Qualification

Advanced Anatomy and Human Biology

Biology

Practical Theology

Contextual Theology

Dyslexia Awareness

El Davies is an author of two books, the second of which is soon to be published. El has an ambition to branch out and write a novel … watch this space …

El has also started a Well-being Therapy business, which incorporates many of the above qualifications and skills, that during her childhood years she was told it would never be possible to attain.

El was written off by many and told she would not achieve any qualifications. El has proved them WRONG! She has achieved far more than was ever thought possible and wants to encourage others that have dyslexia that they can achieve their full potential and to never ever give up!

Printed in Great Britain
by Amazon

82810680R10081